IMAGES
of America

KNOX AUTOMOBILE COMPANY

The author is standing beside a 1907 Knox touring car, the last air-cooled car. Although Knox had seen success with air-cooled engines, the company began using water-cooled engines the following year.

IMAGES
of America

KNOX AUTOMOBILE COMPANY

John Y. Hess

ARCADIA
PUBLISHING

ISBN 978-0-7385-0499-5

Published by Arcadia Publishing
Charleston, South Carolina

Printed in the United States of America

Library of Congress Catalog Card Number: 00108828

For all general information contact Arcadia Publishing at:
Telephone 843-853-2070
Fax 843-853-0044
E-mail sales@arcadiapublishing.com
For customer service and orders:
Toll-Free 1-888-313-2665

Visit us on the Internet at www.arcadiapublishing.com

This was one of three cars built for the Overman Wheel Company in 1897. This car was tested at 25 mph for 100 miles without any problems. Seated are Herman Farr (left) and Harry A. Knox.

CONTENTS

The Springfield Industrial Institute Class of 1894 is shown here. Harry A. Knox is seated on the left in the first row. He graduated at the top of his class and gave the graduation speech to his eleven classmates.

INTRODUCTION

The Knox Automobile Company was a pioneer in the automobile business in New England. It started in 1899 with the manufacture of a three-wheeled, six-horsepower, air-cooled engine. There was no reverse on the transmission, as it could turn a nine-foot circle.

Although Harry A. Knox had only a trade school education, he was an engineering genius. The company built everything from a three-wheeler to tractors, buses, and the ultimate six-cylinder closed car with a 65-horsepower, water-cooled engine. This powerful car won many hill climbs and races. Beginning in 1906, Knox built fire engines that made Springfield, Massachusetts, the first motorized fire department in the country.

The company went out of business in 1927 after building thousands of machines, some of which are shown in this book after having been beautifully restored.

Dedication

I would like to dedicate this book to Billy (Wilfred) Bourque and Harry Holcomb, who lost their lives on August 19, 1909, at the Indianapolis racetrack, and to all the employees of the Knox Automobile Company. Also to the members of the Knox Motor Car Club of America who keep the Knox cars on the road and help keep the name of Knox alive.

Thanks go to my wife, Sheila, who has been a great help throughout this project.

I am happy to be able to share my extensive collection of photographs with you in the history of the Knox Automobile Company.

—John Y. Hess

SPRINGFIELD INDUSTRIAL INSTITUTE,

SPRINGFIELD, MASS.

DAVID ALLEN REED, Pres. L. P. STRONG, Director. MILTON BRADLEY, V. Pres.

Located on State Street between Winchester Park and the N. E. R. R.

• • • • •

TRADE SCHOOL DEPARTMENT.

Day and Evening Instruction in the Trades.

DAY CLASSES in Machine Shop Practice, Plumbing, Cabinet Making, Pattern Making, Brick Laying and Plastering, Stone Cutting and Clay Modeling, Sign and Carriage Painting. Shop equipment of the best. Instructors Skilled, Experienced Mechanics.

• • • • •

ENGINEERING DEPARTMENT. (2 Years' Course.)

For the training of Draughtsmen and others desiring a Practical education. A thorough course in Mathematics, Science, Engineering Subjects, Drawing, and Shop Work.

• • • • •

HIGH SCHOOL DEPARTMENT. (3 Years' Course.)

A TRADE. HIGH SCHOOL STUDIES.

TWENTY HOURS PER WEEK at some Trade. ELEVEN Recitations per Week in High School Studies.

• • • • •

KINDERGARTEN NORMAL DEPARTMENT. (2 Years' Course.)

The Springfield Industrial Institute was one of the first trade schools in the country.

One

The Beginning

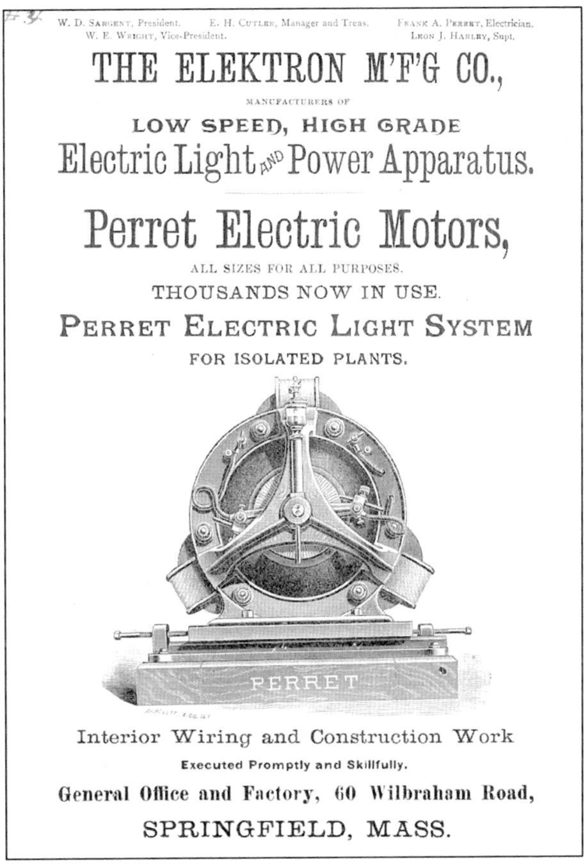

This advertisement is for the company that provided the trade school students with their practical education.

Shown is the third Knox car, built in 1899. Everett H. Barney, a well-known skate manufacturer, owned it. The picture to the rear is Barney seated in the same car. He gave the Knox Automobile Company a blank check when he ordered this car.

This view of the 1899 three-wheel Knox shows Jim Jones Jr., the son of an engineer at Knox. The unique feature on the 1899 Knox is the spindle seat. There was no reverse gear in this vehicle, as it was possible to turn in a 9-foot circle.

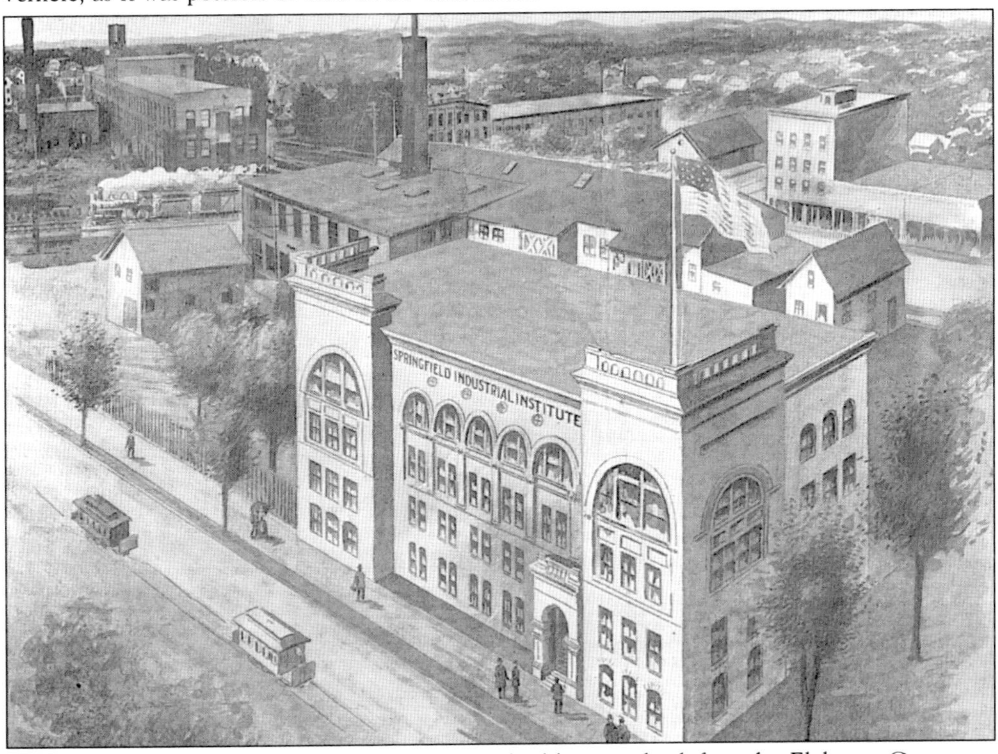

The trade school is shown in this image. The building to the left is the Elektron Company, where the students did their practical work and where the first Knox automobiles were built. The building in the rear center became the Knox Automobile Company.

This Model A, Car No. 1, was built in 1900. The driver is Elmer E. DeGowen, who drove for the company for many years.

In 1901, the first commercial truck was built on a three-wheel chassis and was sold to Smith & Murray, a Springfield dry goods store. They were so impressed with the truck that they traded it in later for a larger truck.

This photograph taken in front of the plant shows the first ten men who worked for the Knox Automobile Company. From left to right are the following: unidentified, Elmore Pennington, unidentified, Herman G. Farr (engineer), Elmer E. DeGowen, Harry A. Knox, unidentified, James Manning, Frederick Craig (first shop superintendent), and unidentified.

Everett H. Barney was one of the first people to purchase a Knox automobile. He was the president of Barney & Berry Skate Company in Springfield. This car is currently on display in the Connecticut Valley Historical Museum at the Quadrangle in Springfield. Barney's personal property and factory were left to the City of Springfield with the understanding that he could live in his house until he passed away.

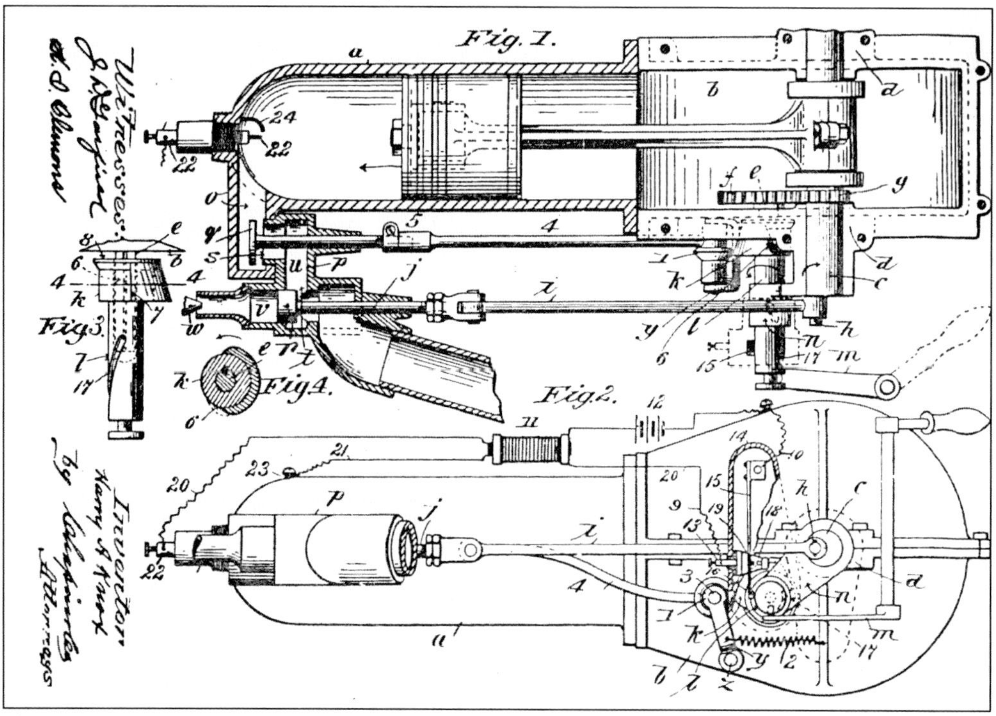

Shown is one of the patents by Harry A. Knox, who held more than 100 of them by the time he died. Although he only had a trade school education, he was considered a genius with a tremendous engineering ability when it came to motor vehicles.

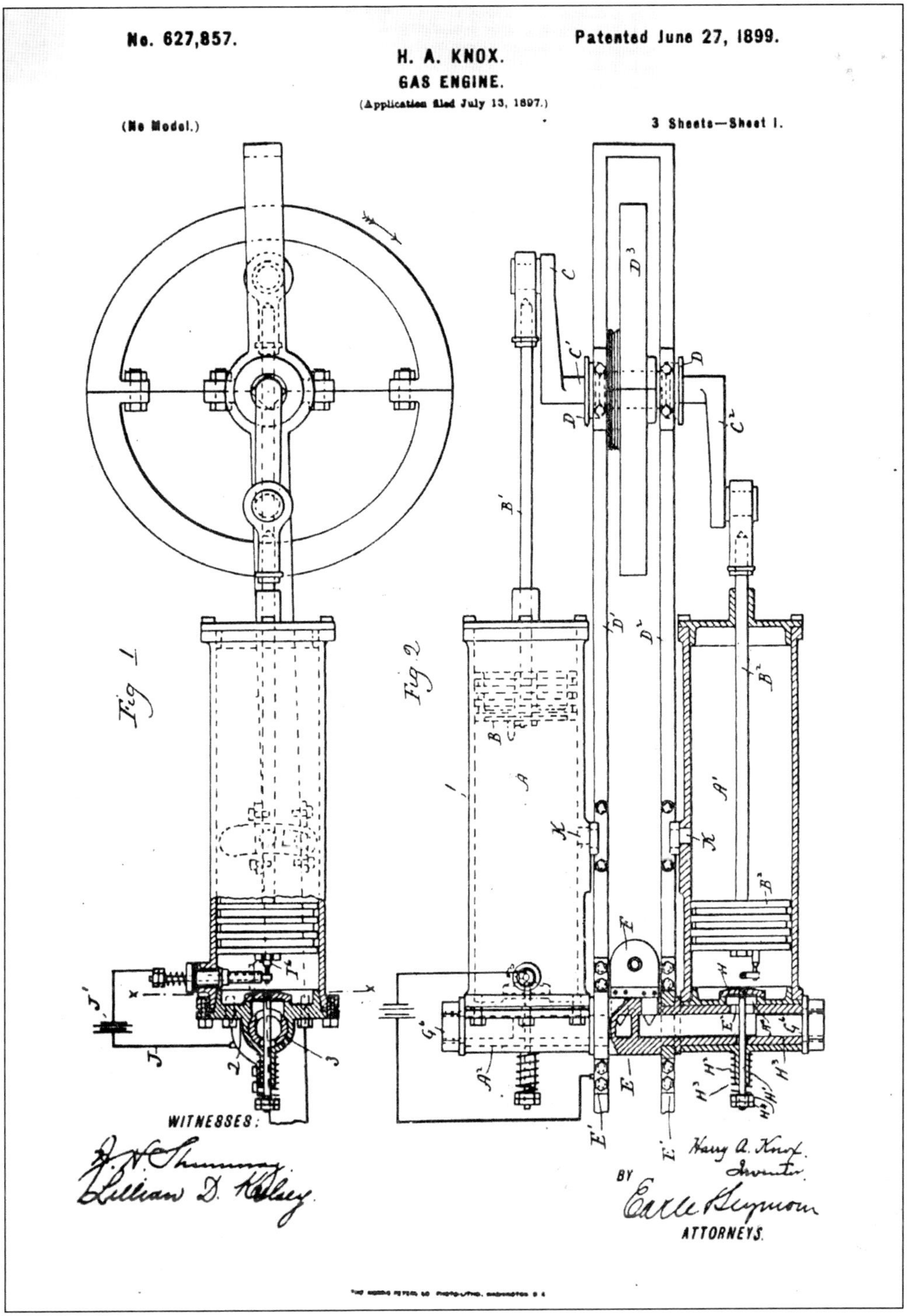

Harry A. Knox was employed by the U.S. government during World War I and developed many patents for tanks and their transmissions.

Another three-wheel Knox carries a couple going for a drive. The car had lever steering; the rod in the front center was the shift lever and gas advance. Note the large flywheel and the chain going to the back axle.

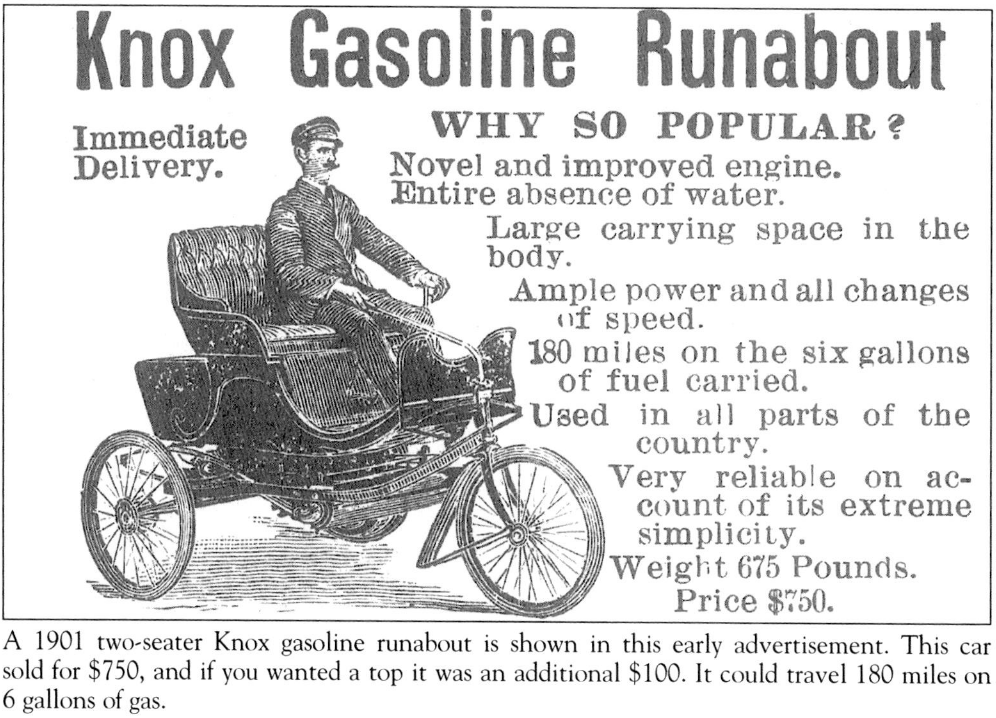

A 1901 two-seater Knox gasoline runabout is shown in this early advertisement. This car sold for $750, and if you wanted a top it was an additional $100. It could travel 180 miles on 6 gallons of gas.

Two

From Three Wheels to Four

This photograph of a 1902 four-wheel Knox shows Harry A. Knox at the steering lever. The men in the front seat are unidentified. Seated beside Knox is Herman Farr. The Cutler brothers, who provided substantial financing for the business, are seated in the rear. This picture was taken on Waltham Avenue in front of the original plant.

This photograph shows a 1902 Knox four wheeler. At the wheel is N.S. Davis, a New York dealer. Notice the spring that goes from the front to the rear axle. This runabout was powered by a single cylinder.

N.S. Davis and family show how the front opened up to carry two more passengers on the 1903 model. Notice the change from wire wheels to artillery wooden wheels, necessary for the added weight of a larger automobile.

This photograph provides a great view of the 1902 chassis, running gear, and single cylinder. The two round cans in the far front are the mufflers. The emergency brake is to the left, with the flywheel a little off center. The crank case cover is to the right of the flywheel, and in front of that is the cylinder shrouded with pins for air cooling.

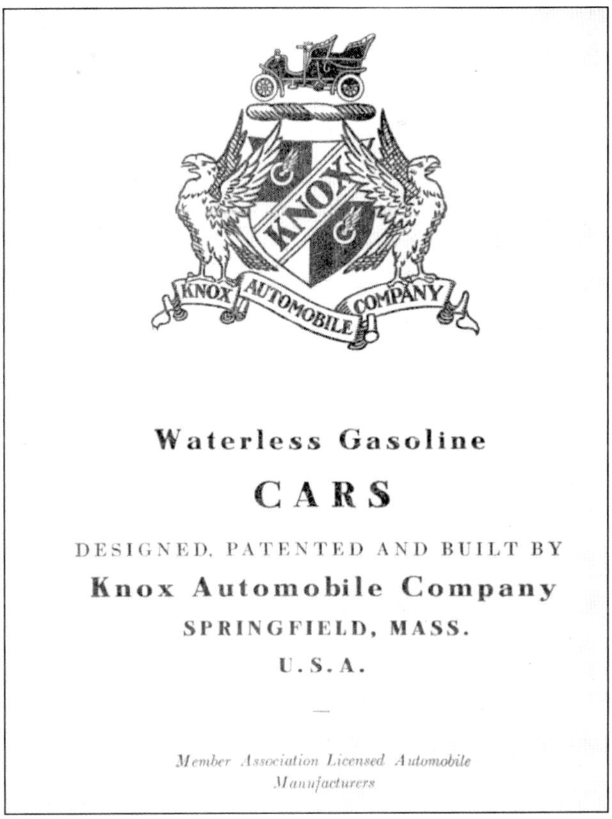

An advertisement shows the Knox logo.

This restored 1902 runabout shows the great style that the Knox cars had. The late Ernie Davignon restored this car.

This photograph of a 1902 chassis shows the one-cylinder engine. Quite evident are the pins, which created 32 inches of surface per inch on the cylinder. It was nicknamed "the porcupine" engine.

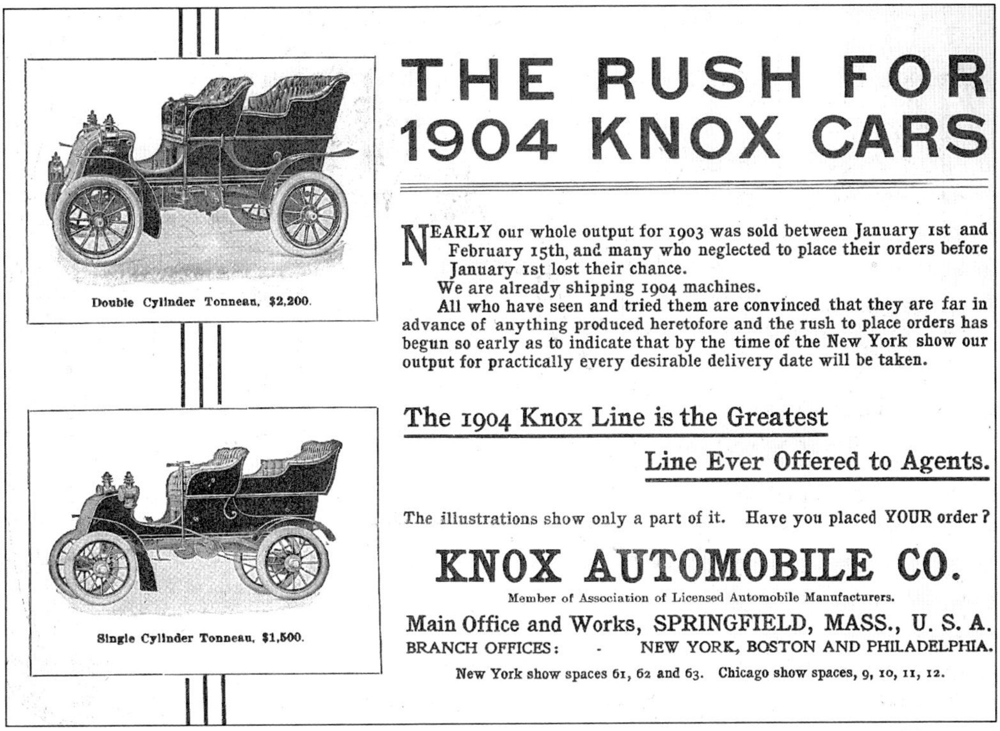

This is an advertisement run by the Knox Company. By 1904, the car company had become well known, and business was booming.

This is the 1904 five-passenger, two-cylinder touring car with lever steering. It was built with the finest leather for the seats, which were surprisingly comfortable.

This advertisement shows the models that were being produced in 1904.

The Knox Company clearly put a great amount of time and thought into its advertisements, and it paid off.

This 1904 touring car was built especially for Elisha Cutler, president of the company at the time. Seated at the steering lever is the author with the late Ernie Davignon.

These 1904 Knox cars and trucks are on a test tour on Wilbraham Road, about a mile from the factory. Most of the factory officers and supervisors were on this test run.

Some of the Knox employees are enjoying a ride on Wilbraham Road. American International College can be seen in the background. Elmore Pennington is driving. Seated in the back seat is William Wright, vice president. The person sitting next to him is unidentified. Pennington worked closely with Harry Knox.

Elmore Pennington is at the steering lever while posing for an upcoming advertisement in the Knox catalog. Note the permanent roof and windshield. The windshield lifted up and latched to the roof when it was not needed. In inclement weather, the side curtains could be rolled down.

This is another model of the 1904 "Tudor," shown in front of the Knox Automobile plant. Notice the windshield latched up to the roof. The tires had tubes and air. The side lights used oil, and the front light was run by acetylene. It had a two-cylinder engine.

This advertisement is for the 1904 Knox, which could be ordered with or without a top.

Two Springfield Gas & Light Company service trucks are shown in front of the company's office at State and Main Streets, c. 1904. Notice the pipe vices on the tailgate. The gas company bought Knox trucks for many years.

The Knox Company organized some of the first motorized parades held in Springfield.

This aerial view shows the Knox plant on the right. The triangular building in the center was the Indian Motocycle building.

Cars line up in front of the Knox plant for a parade on July 4, 1904. This photograph shows the plant before two more floors were added to the existing building.

On June 20 1904, the Knox Company entertained a party of newspapermen. Representatives from Boston, New York, Hartford, and New Haven were taken on a tour of the city. They inspected the factory and had a banquet at the Cooley House. The man standing with the shop coat on is Harry A. Knox.

This photograph taken inside the shop shows some of the car parts. Employees ranged from the very young to much older men. In the back row, fourth from left, is Harry A. Knox. Herman Farr is next to him on the right, and Frederick Craig stands at the far right.

The Knox Company employees had their own band, shown here outside the gate that led into the courtyard.

Three

In and around the Knox Plant

This image shows the original Knox Company plant.

These 1907 cars are completely assembled and ready for shipment. The man standing beside the car on the far left is Gilbert Litle. Standing beside the car on the right is Henry Morse, and seated in the car is Harry Morse.

The office of the Knox Automobile Company is shown in 1904. Seated, from left to right, are Harry A. Knox, Herman G. Farr, Albert Smith, William Wright, and Elisha Cutler. These men comprised the management force of the business.

In the paint department, you can see the 1904 car bodies ready to be painted. Up to 40 coats of paint were applied with a hand rubbing between each coat. Notice the fire pails hanging on the beams. Since the pails had round bottoms and could not stand upright, they were used for fire protection only.

The Knox plant was serviced by the Highland Railroad. This photograph shows some Highland Railroad workers posing in front of one of their engines. Part of the original Knox plant is visible in the background.

This is the Elektron plant, where the first Knox cars were built. The final Knox plant was located across the street. The Otis Elevator Company bought out this company. The final owner of this building was George Hendee, and it became the home of the Indian Motocycle Company in 1910.

This is the main machine shop of the Knox Automobile Company. Note the men's street clothes hanging up and the overhead shafting and belts that ran the machinery.

Note the large machinery that was used in the manufacturing of the automobiles.

This is the engine machine shop. The man in the left foreground is working on the assembly of an engine. You can see the pulleys whirling on the ceiling. The man at the bottom, far left, is Ernest Gramse, a Knox employee for many years.

These happy workers have just returned from a tour in a 1908 Knox. This photograph was taken in the courtyard with Hugo Pac at the steering wheel.

Employees take a ride in a 1904 Knox. Charlie Nadle, in the rear on the left, worked for Knox for many years; he later owned a garage for repairs. This c. 1908 photograph taken on Waltham Avenue shows the Indian Motocycle building in the background.

This photograph shows the tool department where all the engineering drawings were worked out in metal. Ernest Gramse is at the metal-turning lathe. Ernest and his brother, Gusto, worked for Knox for many years. A young boy is running the drill press.

A young men works on a car body in the woodworking shop. Several of the bodies can be seen in progress.

Another young worker in the body shop is working on a 1904 car body.

A man poses in the supply room where the lights for the cars were stored. These side lights used oil and had to be lit at night. At best they were just markers, as they were not bright enough to help the driver see where he was going.

Shown is the truck assembly room with trucks in different stages of assembly. Large electric lights are hanging from the ceiling, and the huge timbers supported the weight of the next floor.

This engine stand was used to move the engines around and up to the chassis for assembly. The Knox Company built a variety of trucks in many styles, including fire rigs.

In the automobile assembly department, work is being performed on a 1910 model. Standing beside the car is Adelbert F. Door, who worked several years for Knox.

A 1904 car is shown with the front panel down. At the steering lever is James H. Jones, one of the Knox engineers. To the left of him is Charlie Martin, another engineer who developed the Knox-Martin tractor and the fifth wheel. Both Jones sons are in the car, one beside his father and the other in the back between the two other boys.

The car on the left is a 1902 model, and the car on the right is a 1903 model with wooden artillery wheels. Engineer Jim Jones was with his two sons and wife out for a ride.

Hiram O. Raymond is shown in a test car on Wilbraham Road in front of the Knox plant. This is a 1902 model with a makeshift body made for testing only. The building to the right became the Duryea Motor Company.

Men from the model shop sit for a portrait. In the front row on the left is John Krampitz. Fourth from the left in the middle row is Albert Chappel, followed by Julian Rand and Ernest Gramse. In the back row, fifth from the left, is Howard G. Parker.

A Knox Model O, 38-horsepower Tonneau has William E. Wright, vice president of the company, at the wheel. The price with a top, magneto, and equipment was $2,950.

Albert Chappel poses with the water pump built for the fire rigs.

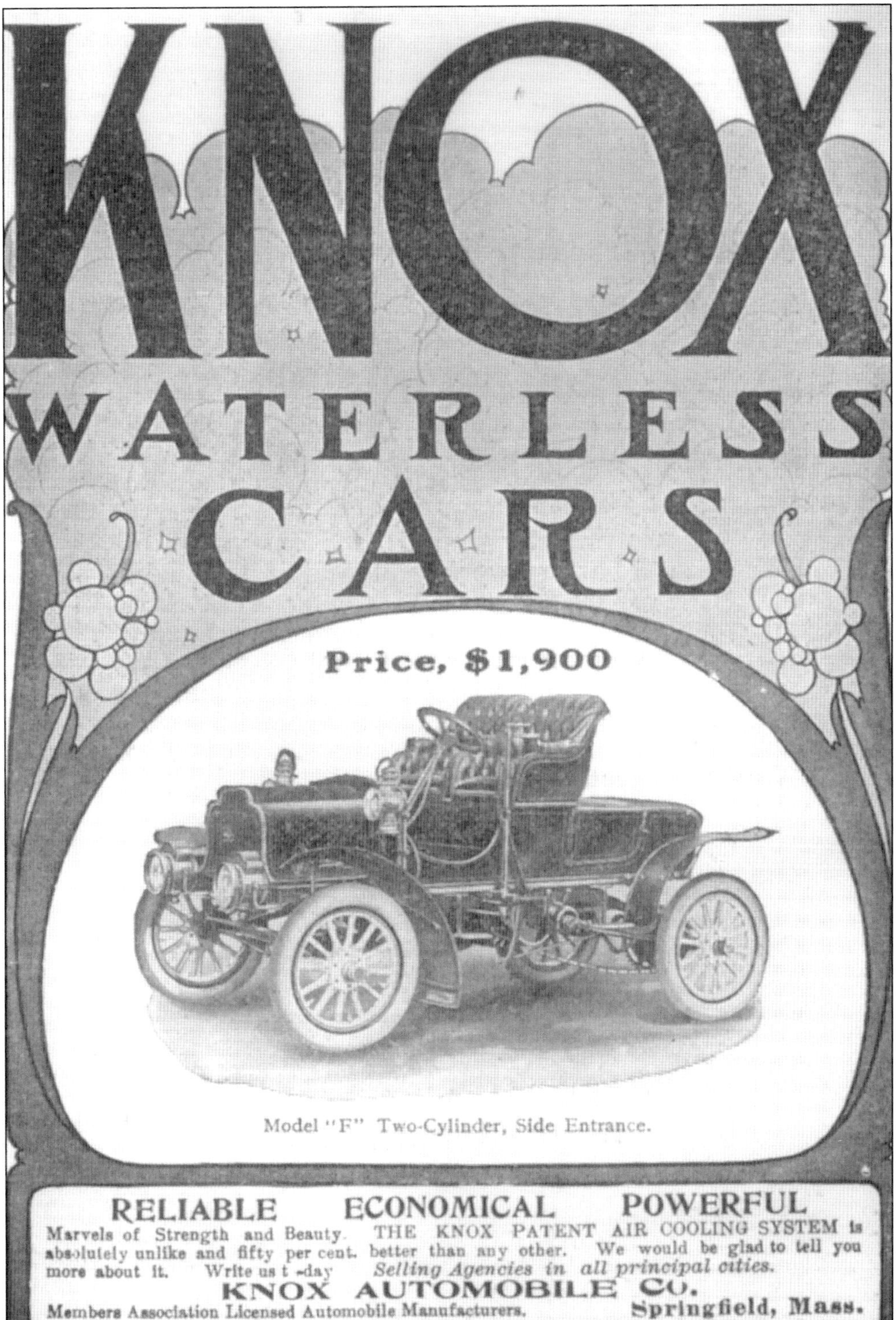

This Knox advertisement is for the 1905 model.

This is C.A. Steiger's first Knox. The car had a hood in front, but the engine was still underneath the body. Steiger owned a department store in Springfield. Mount Tom in Holyoke can be seen to the left.

This advertisement features the 1905 Knox, which still had the air-cooled engine side crank and a 16-horsepower engine.

This price list shows the 1905 cars.

A family is out for a ride in their 1905 touring car with the windshield down and the goggles up. It looks like a nice day for a trip.

A Knox truck was the official baggage wagon on the 1906 Glidden Tour. The license plate number is 09, the official plate number for the Knox Company. The truck is parked in front of the Hotel Richmond.

Two 1907 touring cars are parked across the street from the Knox plant. The Elektron plant is in the background. The trade school class picture on page 6 was taken on the stairs in the background.

This is the air-cooled, four-cylinder engine used in the 1907 cars. The pins are clearly visible on the cylinder, and the lifter rods are exterior on the engine.

Four

Knox Fire Rigs

Knox built fire rigs for towns and cities all over the United States. It was one of the first companies to build fire trucks.

Members of the Springfield Fire Department pose in front of Station 8 at Winchester Park with a Knox hose and ladder truck. Many of the rigs were photographed here, as it was only a block away from the Knox plant.

The Knox-Martin tractor was designed by Charles H. Martin, a Knox employee. Hundreds of these tractors were built to replace the horses. The Walnut Street station of the Springfield Fire Department is in the background.

This close-up view shows the Knox triple combination fire rig. The tank under the seat is the chemical tank. In the center is the pump, which was driven by the rig's engine. At the end of the ladder is the hose basket with Knox script on the end.

This is the reverse side of a triple combination fire rig. The pump was designed by Albert Chappel, a Knox Company engineer.

The Model 9 built by Knox is shown in front of the Winchester Park station in Springfield. The motor was 150 horsepower and could pump 1,000 gallons of water per minute. It was the largest truck the company built.

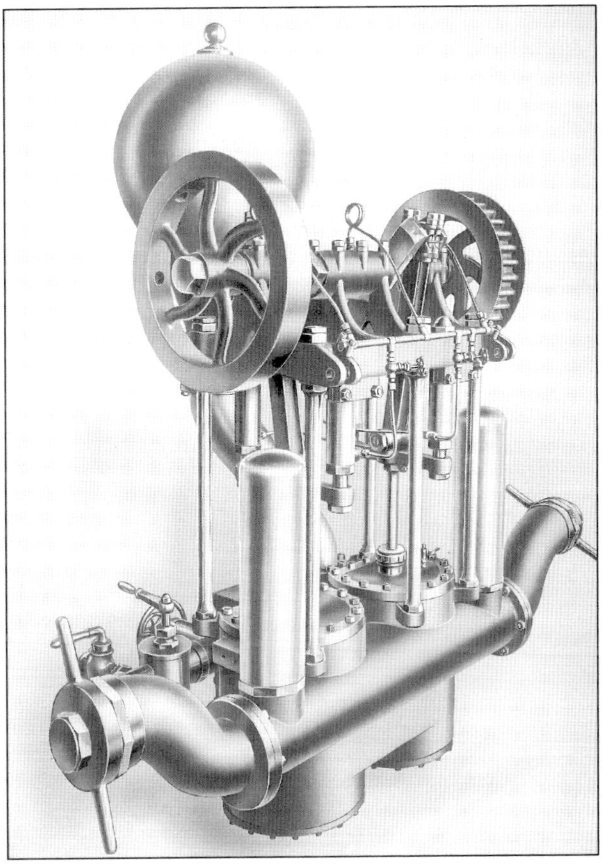

This close-up shows the pump, which was designed in-house, with the big air dome. Also shown are the intake and outlet on the pump.

These Knox fire rigs are lined up on Court Street in Springfield, 1912. The fire department headquarters were nearby. On the left is the steeple of First Church. The tower of the courthouse, built in 1870, is on the right.

This photograph of the Mill Street station shows the Knox rig to the left. The station was built in 1894 and served the city of Springfield until the 1960s. It is now the home of the Tavern Restaurant and the Duryea Transportation Society Museum.

Chief Gordon (right) is shown in the Knox chief's car, purchased in June 1910. The Haverhill Fire Department also bought a 60-horsepower Knox combination chemical and hose rig in 1910 at a cost of $4,500.

Haverhill, along with many other Massachusetts communities, bought Knox fire equipment. Knox was one of the first companies to help motorize the fire rigs from horse-drawn equipment.

Manchester bought this Knox hose and ladder rig, c. 1910. The assistant driver rang the bell behind him all the way to a fire.

Russell "Rusty" Rochford sits at the wheel of the Knox-Martin tractor in front of the Margaret Street station in Springfield. Rusty was a test driver and demonstrator for the Knox Company for many years. He also took the tractor to England and France for demonstration purposes. He started working when he was 16 years old.

This photograph of a Knox Type G combination fire rig was taken on Massachusetts Avenue, Springfield in 1908. Notice the balloon tires and the amount of hose it carried.

Charlie H. Martin, designer of the Knox-Martin tractor, demonstrates it on August 12, 1911. This was the first tractor that was built and the only one with the round nose in front. The Springfield Fire Department had a year to use it before having to pay for it. It proved so successful that the department purchased a second one.

The trustees of Glendale, California, approved the purchase of a 1913 Knox chemical fire rig. In 1914, the city bought its second Knox chemical fire rig for $6,250.

Knox fire rigs are shown in front of the Winchester Park station, c. 1908. About half of the Springfield Fire Department was motorized by this time. In 1915, the whole department was motorized. It was one of the first cities to have a motorized department.

This is the Holyoke fire rig with the body designed by engineers at Knox and the Springfield Fire Department after a Springfield fireman fell from the back of a truck. This was called the "Springfield body." With this type of body, the firefighters could sit on both sides of the back.

In Holyoke, two Knox fire rigs and the Knox chief's car are ready for use. Many cities first motorized with the famous Knox equipment. The change from horses to motorized equipment was very dramatic for these fire companies.

The fire department of Warehouse Point, Connecticut, bought its first motorized rig in 1910. Springfield Metal Body built its body, but the rig was a Knox hose and ladder.

Shown is the first motorized fire rig for Enfield, Connecticut. This rig is one of the early ones with the two-cylinder, air-cooled engine. Its speed was about 25 to 30 mph.

The rig of the Ludlow Fire Department is shown below in a factory image. The Ludlow Manufacturing Associates bought it for firefighting. James Ramsey was scheduled to be the driver, so he went to the Knox plant for a few weeks to learn how to operate it. They had him drive a truck back and forth to Worcester, hauling engines to be ground at the Norton plant.

The City of Ithaca, New York, bought this Knox triple combination fire rig for $8,696 in 1912. It made its last run on April 9, 1944. Ken Soderbeck of Jackson, Michigan, is currently restoring it.

Knox triple combination pump hose and chemical rigs were bought in many New England communities. The City of Chicopee, Massachusetts, purchased this rig in 1912.

This Knox chemical hose and ladder rig was purchased by the fire department in Norwalk, Connecticut, *c.* 1910–1915.

The Gardner Fire Department rig was still in use in 1919, demonstrating its durability. The department also had two Knox-Martin tractors. C.W. Greenwood had the Knox Agency in Gardner and gave their sales commissions to the town, so the Knox Company bid much lower than other companies could offer.

These Knox hose and chemical rigs are parked at the Mill Street station in Springfield. The City of Springfield bought ten of these rigs at one time.

The Knox Automobile Company used postcards for advertising. Shown is Model M-3, a four-cylinder, water-cooled rig with a steel-trussed frame, three-speed selective transmission and a double-side chain drive. It was purchased by the fire department of Melrose, Massachusetts. The tires were 40- by 6-inch Fisk demountable rims with 40-inch and dual tires on the rear wheels. It had two 3-gallon hand extinguishers, ladders, axes, lanterns, bars, and hooks. The wheel base was 145 inches. It could be fitted with one or two 35-gallon chemical tanks.

This postcard of the Knox Automobile Company works in Springfield shows the building before they added two more floors. In the foreground is the Highland Railroad station.

Five

KNOX RACING CARS

Billy Bourque came to Knox in 1903. He worked on engine assembly and then started racing and hill climbing with the Knox. Both Billy and his copilot were killed in 1909 at a car race in Indianapolis.

Another racer for Knox was Charles Basle, shown here in a Knox racecar behind the plant. These racecars were stripped of everything that was not necessary for running.

Charlie Basle, a Knox driver, is shown here at the Merrimack Valley automobile racecourse.

Billy Bourque is at the wheel of a Knox at the Merrimack Valley automobile racecourse.

Model S Six 60, Series A Raceabout, Price $4800

Knox Motor Cars are Winners

RECORDS OF THE KNOX SIX

Unapproached Record of Barney Oldfield and his KNOX Stock Car speaks for itself.

The KNOX six-cylinder owned by Barney Oldfield was the first one of this model built and was contracted for by Mr. Oldfield immediately following his first trial of the car. The following list of events won and records made prove its ability and also again demonstrate the superiority of KNOX features of construction.

SYRACUSE, N. Y. October, 1909. At the State Fair. 1-mile dirt track.
25-Mile record for Stock Cars..........Time 25:40

LOS ANGELES, CAL. Jan. 10th, 1910. mile dirt track.
Won 5-Mile Handicap ....Time 4:46 1-5
" 10-Mile Open for Stock Cars......Time 9:42 3-5
Breaking Coast records.

NEW ORLEANS, LA. Feb. 6-7. Mardi Gras Races. 1-mile dirt track.
Won 25-Mile Handicap ....Time 26:46
" 10-Mile Special Handicap ....Time 9:47
Defeating De Palma in 90-H.P. Fiat.
" 5-Mile Race for Klaw & Erlanger Trophy, valued at $500.00. Car driven by Fred Shaw..........Time 6:5
This Trophy was also won by Mrs. Cuneo in a KNOX GIANT in 1909.

DAYTONA BEACH, FLA. March 22-24.
Won Mile Time Trials................Time 40:35
World's record for Stock Cars at the rate of 89.2 miles per hour.
" 10-Mile Free-For-All...........Time 8:43
" 20-Mile Free-For-All Handicap..Time 18:6

LOS ANGELES, CAL. April 8-18. Speedway Races. One Mile Board Track.
April 8th.
Won 10-Mile Stock Chassis, Class C, 451 to 600 Cubic Inches.............Time 7:49 2-5
WORLD'S RECORD AT THIS TIME —BROKEN AGAIN April 15th and 16th by KNOX.
April 9th.
5-Mile Stock Chassis, Class C, 451-600 Cubic Inches ....Time 3:52:20
WORLD'S STOCK CHASSIS RECORDS.
April 15th.
10-Mile Stock Chassis, Class C........Time 7:22
BREAKING WORLD'S RECORD of April 8th.
April 16th.
10-Mile Stock Chassis, Class C........Time 7:20:66
WORLD'S RECORD — BREAKING one of April 15th.

SALT LAKE CITY, UTAH. April 23. Ingleside Track.
Won 10-Mile Free-for-All............Time 11:08:0
" 2-Mile Handicap Match Race with Darracq and Kerscher....Time 2:15:68

INDIANAPOLIS, IND. May 28th to 30th. Indianapolis Speedway.
Won 5-Mile World's Championship, 600 Cubic Inches.............Time 4:01:2
" 10-Mile World's Championship, 600 Cubic Inches..............Time 7:50:7

KANSAS CITY, MO. June 11th. Elm Ridge Track.
Won 5-Mile Free-for-All ....Time 6:02 1-
" 50-Mile Free-for-All ....Time 56:07

COLUMBUS, O. July 29th. Columbus Driving Park.
Won 25-Mile Free-for-All............Time 26:53 3-

PHILADELPHIA, PA. Aug. 6th. Point Breeze Track.
Won 10-Mile—750 Cubic Inches and under ....Time 11:34 4-
" 6-Hour Race — BREAKING RECORD ....261 MILE

HARTFORD, CONN. Aug. 9th. Charter Oak Park.
Won 5-Mile—600 Cubic Inches.......Time 5:27 2-
" 50-Mile Free-for-All...........Time 51:55
" 5-Mile Free-for-All...........Time 5:20 1-

WORCESTER, MASS. Aug. 11th. Greendale Track.
Won 5-Mile—600 Cubic Inches.......Time 6:52 1-

SEND FOR ILLUSTRATED CATALOGUE

KNOX AUTOMOBILE CO.,

Licensed Under Selden Patents. SPRINGFIELD, MASS.

This advertisement for the Knox Company cites Barney Oldfield's "unapproached record" as a selling point.

Fred Belcher and Bill Jahn, mechanic, raced in 1911 at the Indianapolis racetrack and came in ninth in their first 500-mile race. They won a prize for the fastest lap speed.

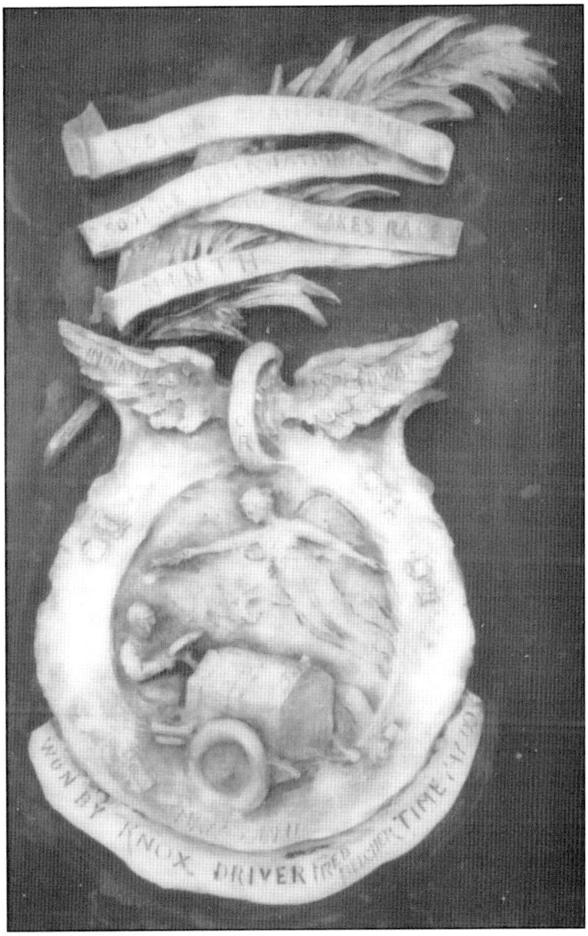

This trophy was won for the fastest lap time of 92 mph at Indianapolis.

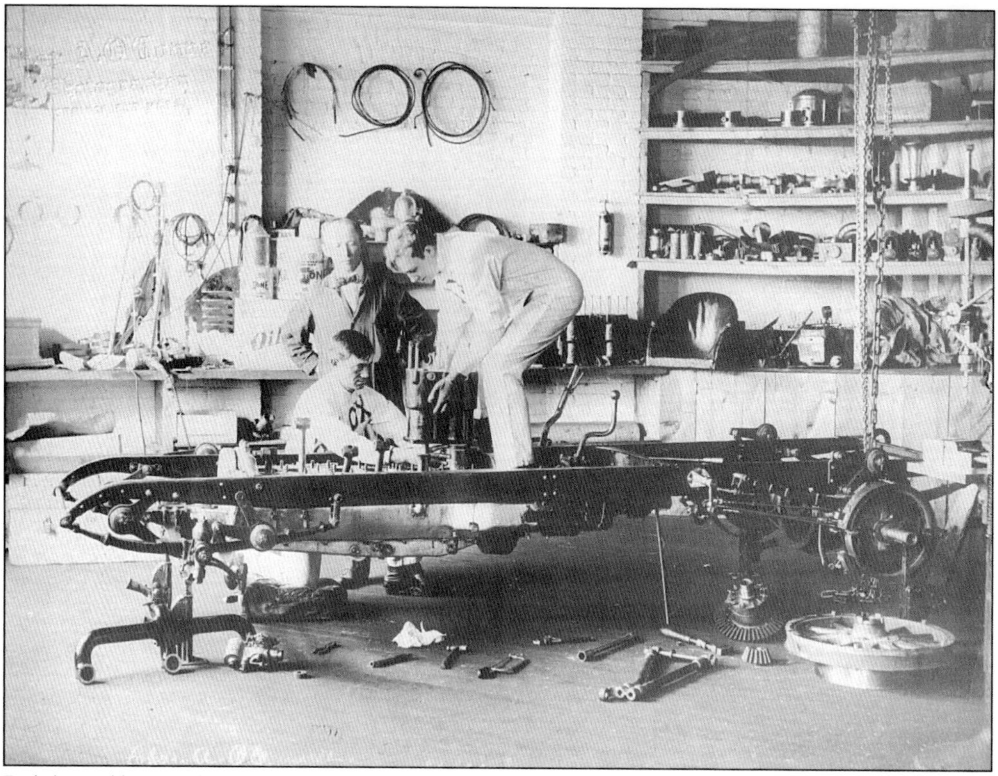

Ralph Mulford and his mechanic, Bill Chandler, strip down the racecar they would use in the 1912 Indianapolis race.

Ralph Mulford and Bill Chandler are shown at the Indianapolis track in 1912.

Charlie Basle and engineer Jim H. Jones pose on Wilbraham Road near the Knox plant. Note the size of the drive chain going to the back wheels.

Al Dennison, another race driver for Knox, is at the wheel. He was at Indianapolis when his friend and coworker Billy Bourque was killed.

Knox Model "M," 4-Cylinder, 48 H. P.

The Model "M" chain drive, 48 H. P. car will be built for 1911 on special order only, requiring 60 days for delivery.

Model "M" is an exceptionally fast stock car. It has the unique distinction of having defeated every prominent make of stock chassis and holds many world's records for speed and hill climbing, including an official speed of 86 miles per hour.

The general specifications follow the Model S, 6-Cylinder very closely and only those details and dimensions which differ will be noted below. The different types will include seven passenger Touring Car, Limousine, Close Coupled, Sport-about and Raceabout in the double chain drive models.

MODEL "M," 48 H. P. SPORTABOUT

With Demi-Tonneau and 106" Wheel Base. Price, Fully Equipped, $4700

This Knox advertisement gives details on the Model M, 48-horsepower sportabout.

Fred W. Belcher climbs a hill in West Poland, Maine, in 1911. If you look closely, you will notice all four wheels are off the ground.

Belcher rides with a passenger in Poland Springs in 1911. After the Knox plant closed, Fred ran his own automobile repair business in Springfield.

Ralph Mulford and his mechanic are getting ready to go to Indianapolis the following day. Notice the wheel disc and the Knox uniforms they are wearing.

Charlie Basle poses for a picture in his Knox racer. Notice the straps holding the hood on. The lights came off in a race, and there was no windshield to protect you from the dust off the track.

Joan Cuneo, a noted racing pioneer, poses at the wheel of her Knox. She came to Springfield on August 19, 1909, and ordered this car to her own specifications. She had grown up in Holyoke.

Joan Cuneo and her husband arrive to pick up her racecar at the Knox plant. She was the only woman to drive in all the Glidden Tours. She won in the car at Mardi Gras races in New Orleans. Joan had two first-place showings, beating several famous drivers.

Six

Knox Trucks

Smith & Murray ordered this 1903 truck, which was a replacement for the first truck, built in 1901. Smith & Murray were the first to buy this model, which was sold to them by Charlie Culver, sales manager.

Notice the mud hooks on the wheels of this 1906 Knox truck. The engine still cranks from the side. A canvas cover is over the engine to keep the pins on the cylinder dry.

A 1906 reliable gasoline, waterless, Knox truck was purchased by the Tim Company. Starting in 1901, several varieties of trucks were being built at the plant.

Two trucks, R7 and R15, were sold to the Indian Motocycle Company in 1912. The Indian plant was directly across the street from the Knox Automobile plant on Wilbraham Road. Both trucks are loaded with boxes of motorcycles for delivery. Knox built trucks up to a 7-ton capacity.

WATERLESS KNOX

COMMERCIAL CARS STAY THE ROUTE.

THE NEW YORK WEEK'S TEST PROVES IT.

"NOTHING succeeds so well as success." Nothing proves the worth of a commercial car so well as the success of it in actual road test. Three Knox cars entered the New York "Commercial Vehicle Test" for the week ending April 9. They were employed by the American Express Co. and the Wescott Express Co. all over New York City and to Long Island for general deliveries. Each car accomplished about three times as much as each horse drawn vehicle and **went the entire test week without a single interruption.**

THE MORAL IS PLAIN:

If You Want the Commercial "Car That Obviates the Tow"

SELECT THE KNOX.

You see the Knox has the only high power engine successfully and automatically cooled by air. No water to freeze in winter and no overheating in summer. The Knox air cooling system does it. What others ATTEMPT to do, the Knox DOES.

BETTER SEND FOR OUR BEAUTIFULLY ILLUSTRATED CATALOGUE AND LEARN WHY.

KNOX AUTOMOBILE CO., Springfield, Mass.

Members of Association of Licensed Automobile Manufacturers.

Selling Agencies in All Principal Cities.

This is a typical Knox Automobile Company advertisement.

The F.A. Towne delivery truck was the faithful 1904 vintage. The company was located in Ludlow, Massachusetts.

The Springfield Gas Light Company bought several trucks starting in 1904. This is a 1909 pickup. Sitting on the running board is Mr. Bergamini, a longtime employee of the Springfield Gas Light Company.

This 1906 truck, with a carrying capacity of 6,000 pounds, is loaded with a lathe. By this time, the steering was done by a wheel rather than a lever.

Workers from the Springfield Water Works are loading water main pipe onto this Knox platform truck. You can also see an electric crane for loading. To the left is the Knox Automobile plant. The truck driver is S. Brooks, and the man in the back is C.E. Bose.

A 1903 Knox truck with a single-cylinder air-cooled engine is pictured here. This model was used mainly for light duty work.

This 1904 model, built for the Edison Light Company, was a two-cylinder, 16-horsepower truck.

This closed 1904 Knox truck was built for the Ostermoor Mattress Company. It was a two-cylinder, air-cooled engine with 16 horsepower. This elaborate paint job was used on many of the trucks.

A 1904 Knox truck built for the John T. Connor Corporation, wholesale grocers. This model had lever steering and a rack body with a canvas top and side curtains, which could be rolled down in inclement weather.

This Knox delivery truck was bought by the Jordan-Marsh Company of Boston. The 1904 model chassis had lever steering and a two-cylinder, air-cooled engine. A company driver accompanied the truck for its delivery to Boston. The company was so pleased with the truck that they ordered several more.

A 1906 Knox stake body truck also has the two-cylinder air-cooled engine. Just imagine driving this truck in the winter.

KNOX WINS

on Shingle Hill, New Haven

Fred Belcher, driving his Knox 6-cylinder, 60-h. p. stock car, WON the 451-600-cu. in. piston displacement event in the fast time of 52.75 secs. from a large field of noted cars and racing pilots.

Jack Coffey, driving a Knox 4-cylinder, 40-h. p. stock car, made the second best time in the 301 to 450-cu. in. event.
In the big race of the meet—the free for all—Belcher came in second, being defeated only by a 200-h. p. Fiat and winning from a field of a dozen racing cars. In this event the Knox was the winning stock car.

These continual winnings point to the right construction, ample power and ability to stand the strains.

Buy a Knox and You Buy a Winner

KNOX AUTOMOBILE CO.

SPRINGFIELD, MASS.

This advertisement shows that winning races was good for business.

In the White Mountains on the Glidden Tour, Charles Culver, sales manager for Knox, sits next to the driver in this 1906 photograph.

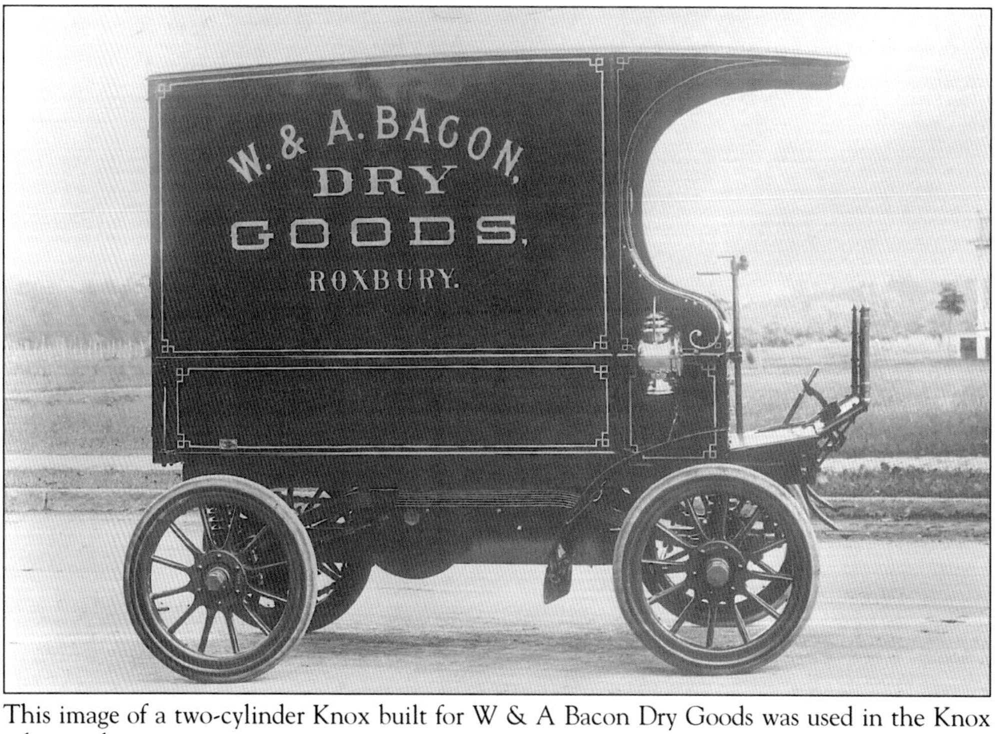

This image of a two-cylinder Knox built for W & A Bacon Dry Goods was used in the Knox sales catalogs.

Seven

Knox Buses

This 1906 Holyoke and Belchertown auto bus was run by Elmore Pennington, a former Knox employee.

W. E. WRIGHT
Vice-President and General Manager

ALBERT E. SMITH
Assistant Treasurer

H. G. FARR
Mechanical Engineer

This image shows William E. Wright, vice president and general manager; Albert E. Smith, assistant treasurer; and Herman Farr, mechanical engineer.

The first buses were built in 1906. This was a seven-passenger vehicle and had a canvas top and curtains that could be unrolled in bad weather. However, there was no windshield for the driver.

In 1906, a six-passenger automobile was built for the Fitchburg Auto Transit Company. The seats were padded with horsehair and the springs were covered with the best leather available.

Knox came a long way with this closed bus. Some of these were exported to Japan. Notice the ladder so the driver could get to the roof for the baggage storage.

A twelve-passenger bus is ready for shipment. You can see the steps that were used to get to the seats. Also shown is the emergency brake on the outside of the frame by the driver's seat.

This bus has a different seating arrangement with the seats behind the driver and the rest along the sides. This was built for the Bass Rocks Motor Line.

Built for the Loudon Road Auto-Bus Lines, this bus had a design that was different from previous ones—you would enter from the rear and the seats were on both sides. Notice the Knox emblem on the side of the front seat.

Built for the West Indies Transportation Company, this bus had seats made of wooden slats instead of leather. The wood stood up better in this area because of the dampness. Notice the two sets of stairs in front and back of the rear wheel.

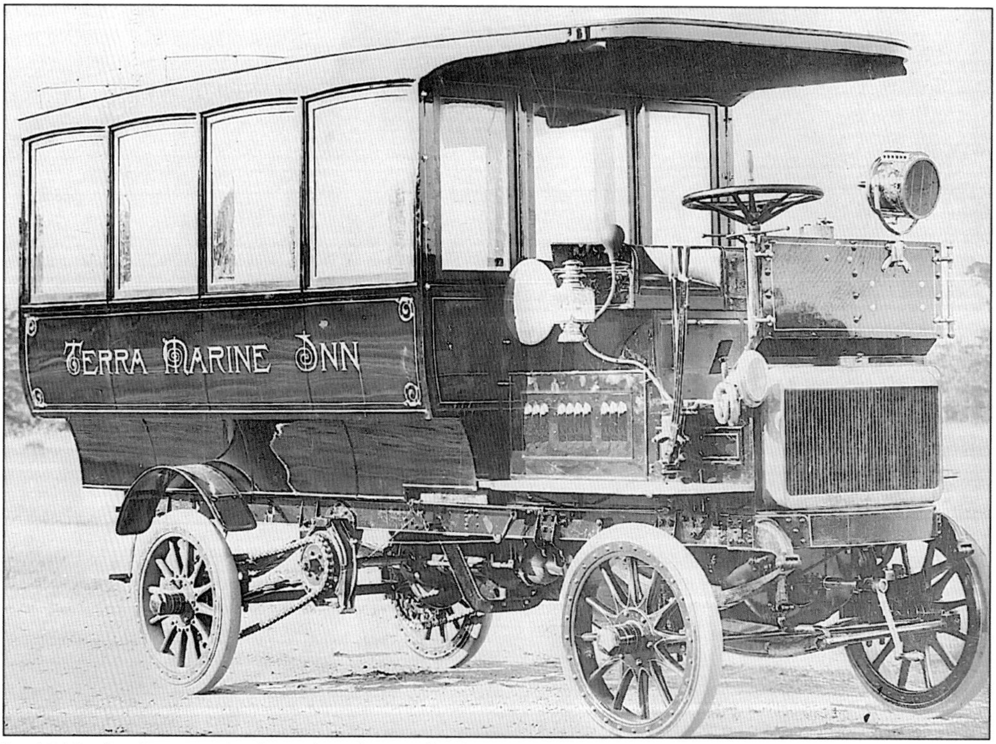

In 1911, this bus was built with a four-cylinder, water-cooled engine for the Terra Marine Inn. It was closed in with windows that dropped into pockets under the window. The entrance was from the rear of the bus.

This is a four-cylinder, water-cooled engine bus, which could be entered from both sides. There were no curtains for bad weather. This model had a 15-person capacity.

The ultimate for 1911 was a closed bus and entrance behind the driver where you would pay upon entering. Even the driver was enclosed in this model. It also had a hand rail at the entrance. This one was used on the Orange Street line.

Eight

Cars and Later Models

This advertisement shows a 1911 King of the Road touring car.

In 1912, Knox cars began to look more like contemporary cars, with doors and windows and a top and windshield.

1912 KNOX MODEL "R" TOURING CAR, SERIES B

4-Cylinder, 40 H. P., Five or Seven Passenger. Price Fully Equipped, $3,500

The aim of this model is comfort and convenience. The clean, straight lines of body and running board, the tool carrier chambers, accessible without disturbing passengers, and the easy exit from the driving seat are progressive features tourists appreciate. The equipment is exceptionally large.

This model will be furnished with the new 4-cylinder long stroke motor having 5" bore and 5½" stroke, for $100 extra.

SPECIFICATIONS

Motor: Four cylinder, cast separately, 5" bore and 4¾" stroke. Made with detachable heads, valves in the head. 40 H. P., A. L. A. M. rating.

Transmission: KNOX selective type, 3 speeds forward and one reverse, on imported annular ball bearings. Emergency brake and gear lever mounted in center of car. Right hand position of same if desired.

Clutch: KNOX three plate with cork inserts.

Drive: Straight line, shaft and bevel gears.

Ignition: Double ignition system, battery and magneto. Two complete systems, including separate switches.

Lubrication: De Dion system, pumped from well in crank case.

Gasoline Tank: 18 gallons capacity, located under front seats. Four-way valve placed conveniently for controlling gasoline supply, drainage, pressure, etc.

Steering: Irreversible type, double thread. Adjustable for wear. All parts of high grade alloy steel. 18" mahogany steering wheel.

Frames: Cold pressed alloy steel, heavy gauge, properly heat treated.

Springs: Front 42". Rear 50". Tough alloy steel. Semi-elliptic front and ¾ scroll elliptic rear. Fitted with shock absorbers.

SPECIFICATIONS

Wheel Base: 122". **Tread:** 56". **Wheels:** Wood artillery type.

Tire and Rim Equipment: 36 x 4½" Fisk bolted-on type with Fisk demountable rims as regular equipment, with an option of Universal rims and clincher tires.

Front Axle: Tough alloy steel, "I" beam type. Timken bearings in pivots and wheels.

Rear Axle: KNOX full-floating type, mounted on imported annular ball bearings, detachable high grade alloy steel shafts. Complete differential easily and quickly demounted.

Brakes: Both acting on double rear wheel drums. Service brake is of the contracting band type, operated by foot pedal. Emergency brake is of the expanding type, a hand lever pull brake. Both have equalizers.

Tool Boxes: Arranged along running board. Water tight, neat and compact.

Body: Sheet aluminum and steel over wooden frames. Designed and manufactured in KNOX body works.

Colors: Battleship gray, Brewster and Thistle green, Blue, Royal purple, Wine, Maroon, Dark carmine, KNOX red, Tan and Chocolate brown.

Upholstery: Hand buffed leather in colors to match painting.

Trimmings: Nickel plated or brass throughout.

Equipment

Top complete with side curtains and top slip, metal bound glass front, Jones 60-mile speedometer, clock, two 8" headlights, combination oil and electric side lamps, and rear lamp wired with 6-70 Witherbee storage battery, Prest-O-Lite tank, combination bulb and electric horn, Bosch magneto with cover, Hartford motor driven tire pump, gasoline gauge, four-way gasoline cock, shock absorbers, coat rail, folding foot rail for tonneau, foot rail for left hand front seat, floor mat, Fisk demountable tires and rims, extra Fisk rim, tire cover, special tire carrier trunk, baggage rack, number plate bracket, steering knuckle covers, new style running board chambers, patent oil can holder, jack, hand tire pump, tire repair kit, full set of tools.

The Portland Company in Maine was an agency for the Knox Automobile Company. Shown here are some 1910 models that had just been delivered to the agency.

This is a completely closed car with a six-cylinder engine. The back seat is closed off from the driver's seat. Notice that the tires have no tread on them.

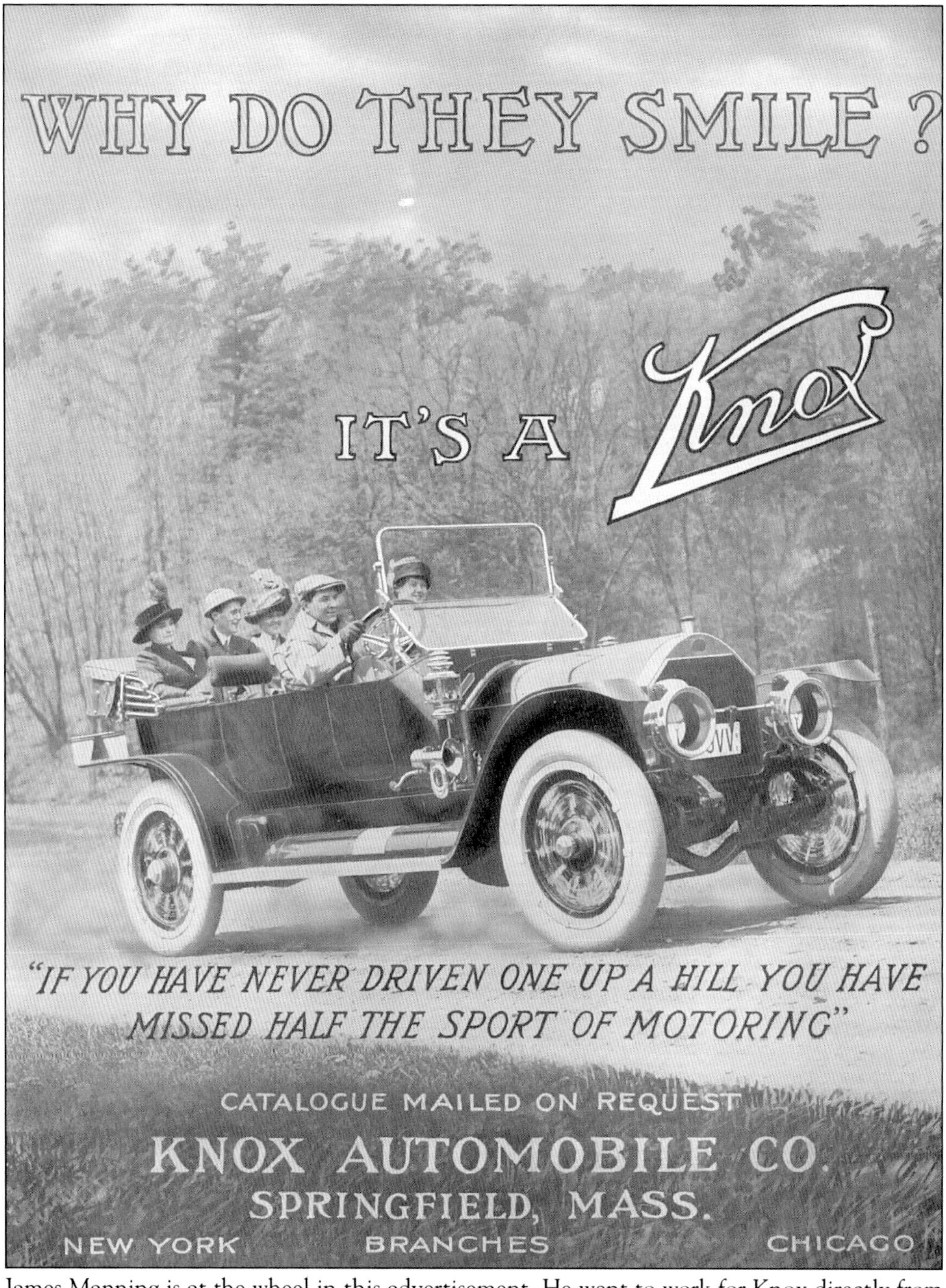

James Manning is at the wheel in this advertisement. He went to work for Knox directly from Springfield High School and before long was in charge of sales. James worked in the main office until the plant closed. He worked at Knox longer than any other company employee.

The acetylene tank on the running board is the gas for the headlights, with the toolbox just behind it. The two side lights used oil for fuel. This car has beautiful leather upholstery with diamond pleats and buttons.

This is the 1911 six-cylinder, water-cooled engine. Notice the teeth on the flywheel. By that time, the cars had starters so that cranking was no longer necessary.

This is an advertisement for the 1911 model Knox. "Best by Test" was a company slogan.

This is the booth at the New York Car Show, which was usually held in January. Five Knox models were on display, plus an engine on the stand. Knox took many orders at the automobile shows.

This Model O sportabout with a single rumble seat was equipped with a top and magneto. It sold for $2,850.

William E. Wright, the vice president of Knox, is in a 38-horsepower Model O. The total price with magneto and equipment was $2,950. This model also came with a horn, toolbox on the running board, and a bulb horn.

Touring Mount Washington on the Glidden Tour are, from left to right, William E. Wright at the wheel, Albert Dennison beside him, Charlie Culver, and Elisha Cutler. The women in the back seat are unidentified.

Elmore Pennington is at the wheel of this six-cylinder, seven-passenger limousine. The engine was in the 60-horsepower range.

Two large Knoxes are parked at Winchester Square in front of the Van Der Hyden luxury apartments. The Knox Company provided several cars for the Victory Parade on July 4, 1919.

This is the famous Knox Vanderbilt Cup car shown at the corner of Waltham Avenue and Wilbraham Road. The Indian Motocycle building can be seen in the background. Mabel Webber, prima donna of the Merry Widow Company is seated in the car. The holes in the hood of the car blew exhaust directly from the engine.

This the 1913 car in front of the George Walter Smith Art Museum in Springfield. The heavy oak doors and cut glass made a beautiful background for these magnificent cars.

Nine

Four-Wheel Tractors and Company Personnel

The Knox four-wheel tractor was equipped with the fifth wheel. The Martin fifth wheel connection was the beginning of the tractor-trailer combination, which is basically the same today. Engineering for this began in 1915. The Knox Company license plate, No. 09, is visible here. This tractor also had hydraulic brakes.

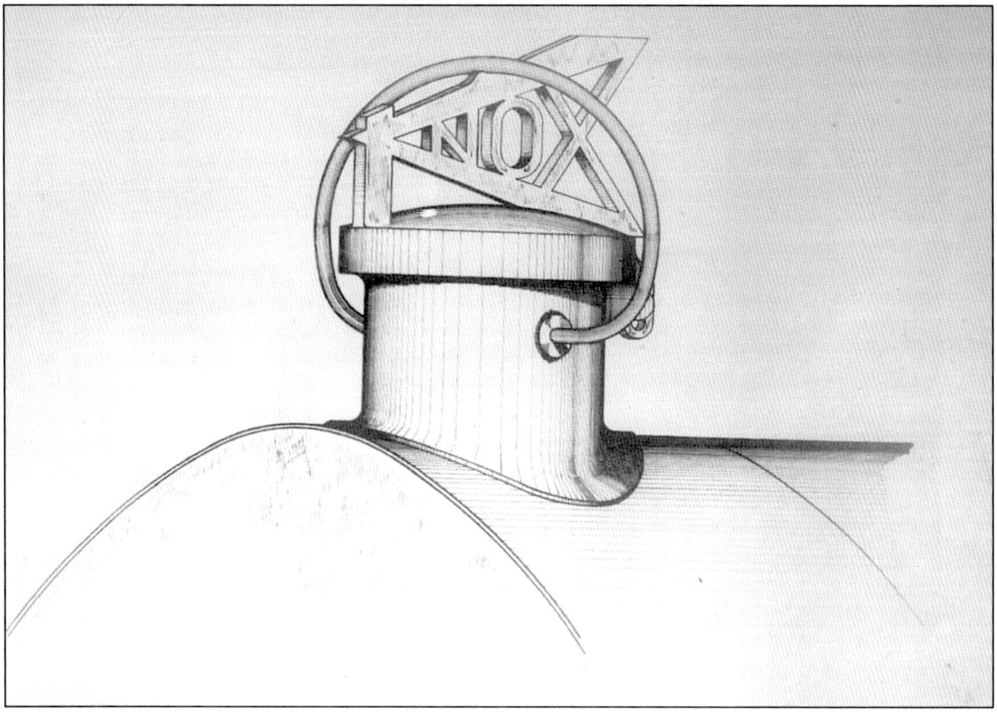

The fancy radiator cap on the four-wheel tractor is shown here. The Borden Milk Company replaced all its horses with these tractors and trailers.

This side view of the Knox four-wheel tractor shows the location of the fifth wheel. It also had the usual canvas top and side curtains. It was a very powerful tractor.

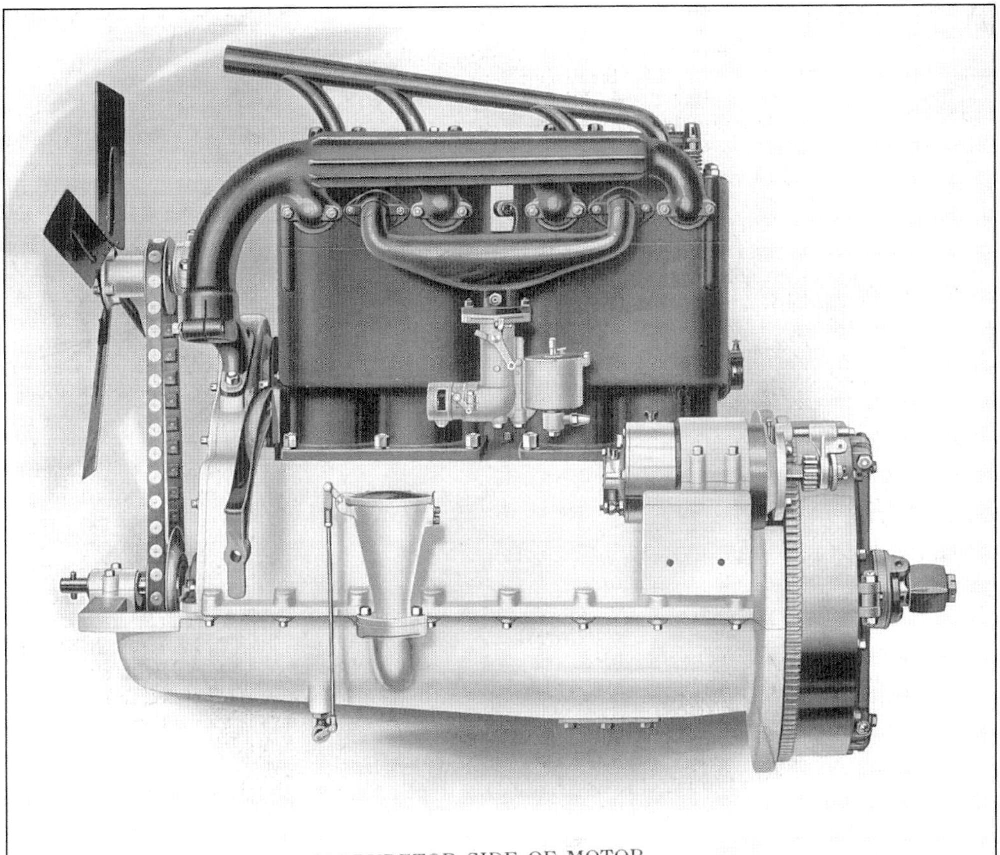

CARBURETOR SIDE OF MOTOR

This engine went into the four-wheel tractor. The company went through money problems, and it was reorganized as Knox Motor Associates of Springfield in 1914.

This blotter was used as an advertisement for a new tractor. The tractor was capable of hauling 15 to 20 tons.

C. L. GOODHUE, Pres. W. E. WRIGHT, V. Pres. A. N. MAYO, Treas. ALBERT E. SMITH, Asst. Treas. E. O. SUTTON, Clerk. H. G. FARR, M. E.

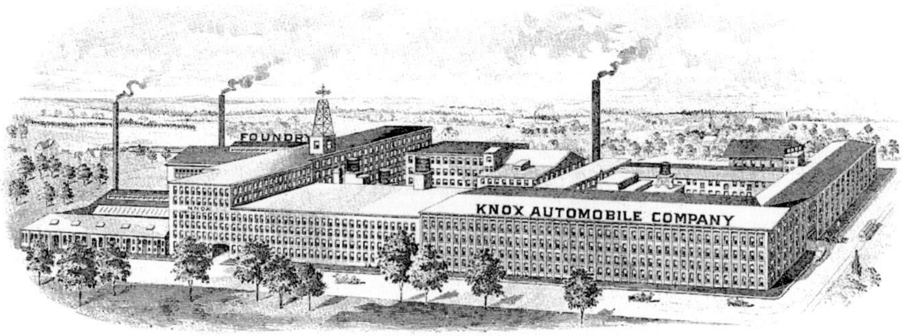

KNOX AUTOMOBILE COMPANY,

WHEN REPLYING PLEASE REFER TO THESE INITIALS P. L. H.

SPRINGFIELD, MASS. April 29, 1912.

ADDRESS ALL COMMUNICATIONS TO THE COMPANY.

Mr. Geo. H. Calder,

Lancaster, Pa.

Dear Sir:

Kindly send us circular matter and quote us price on your #2 emery wheel dressers, and advise if you have any agents in our territory.

Yours very truly,

KNOX AUTOMOBILE COMPANY.

P. L. Hicks

Purchasing Agent.

HH

This correspondence shows the company letterhead.

CLEAN SWEEP

BY THE

KNOX

AT THE

Poland Spring Hill Climb, Saturday, June 17, 1911

Adds FOUR More VICTORIES

TO THE LONG LIST OF KNOX WINNINGS

On the most difficult automobile hill in Maine, Fred Belcher, driving the big Knox Six, made the 2-3 mile climb in the record time of 50 seconds flat and also won his class event from a good field.

Jack Coffee, driving the Knox 4-cylinder car WON the two events in which his car was entered.

AS USUAL the Knox takes the Lion's share of the Prizes.

IT'S IN THE MOTOR AND DESIGN

KNOX AUTOMOBILE CO

SPRINGFIELD, MASS.

The company's advertisements were very effective in promoting automobiles. This is one of the reasons companies competed in hill climbs and races.

In 1917, another product was introduced by the Knox Motors Associates known as a traction unit, which converted a used car into a tractor for hauling trailers.

Charles Culver, Knox sales manager, and his wife are out for a ride in a 1905 car. The people in the back seat are unidentified.

The author talks with Herman Munger (left), a former Knox employee, in November 1985. Mr. Munger was 92 years old at the time.

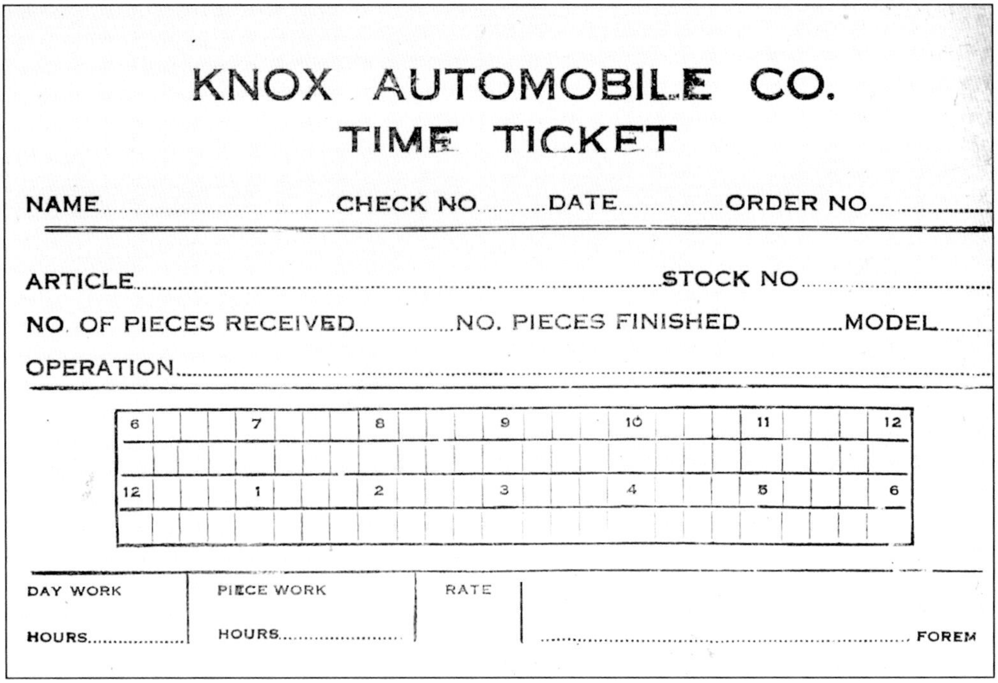

KNOX AUTOMOBILE CO.

TIME TICKET

NAME .... CHECK NO .... DATE .... ORDER NO ....

ARTICLE .... STOCK NO ....

NO. OF PIECES RECEIVED .... NO. PIECES FINISHED .... MODEL ....

OPERATION ....

6	7	8	9	10	11	12
12	1	2	3	4	5	6

DAY WORK	PIECE WORK	RATE	
HOURS	HOURS		.... FOREM

Shown is a time ticket used by Knox employees.

A Knox-Martin tractor hauls two 50-ton houses tied together. These houses were moved about a half mile away when the Elektron plant was expanded.

Knox employee Frank Tunstall hauls a load of potatoes.

Barney Oldfield poses in his six-cylinder racecar that he had Knox build for him in 1909. This was the beginning of the six-cylinder racers.

This Knox advertisement uses Barney Oldfield's records on the track.

Knox employee Elmore Pennington poses with his 1903 runabout in 1945.

A Knox fire rig is seen in the test stand at Watershops Pond. The driver is Rusty Rochford. Standing, from left to right, are two unidentified men; Fred Perkins; and his father, Charles Perkins. Charles was in charge of the department involved in the construction of fire rigs.

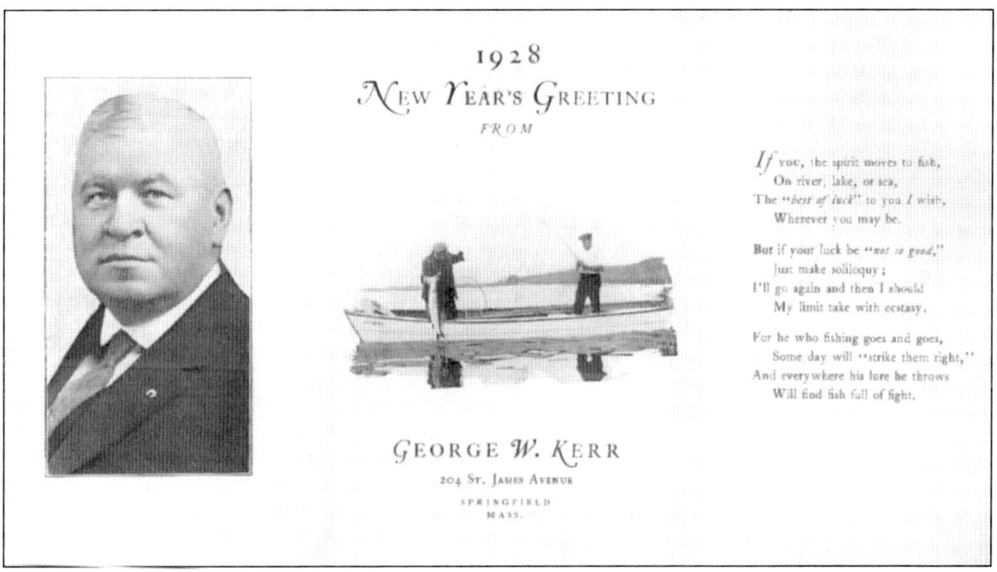

George W. Kerr was the body designer for Knox, Stevens-Duryea, and Rolls-Royce.

This Knox-Martin tractor is in New York City pulling a 20-ton garbage trailer. Charlie Martin is standing on the trailer.

PLANT OF THE KNOX MOTORS COMPANY
Recently absorbed and to be greatly expanded by the Militor Corporation

This image shows the Knox plant at the end of its business days. In 1940 Milton Bradley Company, Brockway-Smith, and a chemical company subdivided the plant.

FACTORY NOTICE — No. 134

Date September 11th, *191* 4. *Subject* NOTICE TO EMPLOYEES.

It has been called to my attention at various times that our employees are not as careful as they should be in their conversation outside of the Factory. This has been particularly noticeable since work started on the Model 35 tractor. We are very open in our Experimental Dept., doing the work where all of the men watch progress etc., expecting, of course, that they will respect their knowledge of such work as we may be putting through and keep it confidential. I want each employee to feel that we have confidence in his ability to keep to himself all methods, experimental work, records, etc. which may be in process or in use throughout the Factory, remembering that it is for the employees benefit as well as for our benefit as a whole that such information be kept within our doors.

Please take due notice of this and govern yourselves accordingly.

J. M. Collins.
Supt.

FORM F-1

This is a factory notice to employees written by John M. Collins, who was the assistant superintendent and purchasing agent. He left the company in 1914 to take a position with the Moore Drop Forge Company. By 1932, Collins was treasurer and in 1938 became president of Moore Drop.

A monthly pass for the Louisiana Purchase Exposition in 1904 shows John M. Collins.

Sitting in the back seat are an unidentified man (left) and William E. Wright. John M. Collins (driving) and Charlie Culver are in the front seat. The car is a 1909 model with a four-cylinder, water-cooled engine.

John M. Collins (with cap) is seen here in a 1903 runabout.

This is the patch of the Knox Motor Car Club of America, which consists of Knox car owners and interested people. We keep the name of Knox alive. The patch, designed by the author, features the Knox logo with "Knox Motor-Car Club" replacing "Knox Automobile Company."